THE PATH TO LONG-TERM INVESTMENT

Unveiling the Truth About Investments, Avoiding Get-Rich-Quick Schemes, and Building Sustainable Wealth for a Secure Future

Jerry R. Schaefer

TABLE OF CONTENTS

Introduction

Welcome to "Investing with Wisdom: Navigating the Financial Landscape." In this journey, we unravel the complexities of investing, focusing on practical insights to shield you from the allure of get-rich-quick schemes. As we delve into the nuances of financial strategies, our aim is to equip you with the knowledge needed to make informed decisions, steering clear of pitfalls and embracing the true potential of responsible investing.

The Purpose of Investing

Investing, a beacon beckoning towards financial prosperity, holds the promise of a secure future. Yet, within this promise lies a labyrinth of complexities, often obscured by the dazzle of extravagant claims and market exuberance. To embark on this journey with wisdom, one must first decipher the true purpose of investing and embrace the need for financial responsibility.

At its core, investing is not a magic wand capable of transforming financial fortunes overnight. Rather, it serves as a patient ally, steadily accumulating wealth over time. The primary purpose lies in bridging the gap between our current financial state and the desired future – be it retirement, financial independence, or other long-term goals. Investing, when approached with prudence, becomes a powerful tool for building wealth over the years.

However, as the landscape evolves, so do the temptations. The rise of cryptocurrencies, NFTs, and enticing trading courses has added a layer of complexity, tempting investors with the allure of quick and massive returns. It is crucial to distinguish between legitimate investment opportunities and speculative ventures that often lead to disappointment.

The Need for Financial Responsibility

In the pursuit of financial well-being, responsibility becomes the cornerstone. This responsibility manifests in two fundamental aspects – saving and investing. The Spectrum Group Survey, which delved into the habits of individuals with net worth between $100,000 and $1 million, unveiled a recurring theme among successful households. A dedicated and regular savings program emerged as a crucial factor, underscoring the significance of prudent spending habits.

Saving, often overshadowed by the allure of high-return investments, is the unsung hero of financial success. The ultra-high net worth individuals, according to the same survey, scored even higher on valuing a dedicated savings program. This dispels the myth that investing alone can pave the way to affluence. The ability to resist impulsive spending and diligently save lays the groundwork for sustainable financial growth.

While saving builds the foundation, investing propels the journey forward. However, it demands a cautious approach, steering clear of the rampant market exuberance that characterizes certain periods. Cryptocurrencies and NFTs, propelled by hype, often entice investors with promises of astronomical returns. Herein lies the need for financial responsibility – the ability to discern between genuine opportunities and speculative traps.

Understanding the average returns of the stock market, typically around 10%, underscores the importance of realistic expectations. This return, while respectable, requires careful consideration of taxes and inflation, which significantly diminish the actual gains. Acknowledging these factors emphasizes the need for long-term commitment and patience in the realm of investing.

In the age of information overload, it becomes imperative to sift through marketing tactics that promise quick wealth. The allure of overnight success stories may captivate, but it's essential to recognize these as exceptions rather than the rule. True financial growth stems from a combination of active income, prudent saving, and strategic investing over an extended period.

The intersection of saving and investing becomes the sweet spot for financial responsibility. It's not a matter of choosing one over the other but rather understanding how they complement each other. The myth that investing is a substitute for saving dissipates when we scrutinize the habits of those who have successfully amassed wealth. The millionaire and ultra-high net worth groups, as revealed by the survey, score high on both saving and investing, dispelling the notion of mutual exclusivity.

In essence, the purpose of investing intertwines with the need for financial responsibility. It's a dynamic interplay where saving provides the fuel, and investing becomes the engine propelling financial growth. This synergy, however, demands a discerning eye and a commitment to long-term principles. As we navigate the chapters ahead, the journey unfolds as a pursuit not just of wealth but of financial wisdom and resilience.

Chapter 1: Recognizing Market Exuberance

Navigating the turbulent waters of investing requires a keen awareness of market exuberance. Chapter 1 sheds light on recognizing the signs and symptoms of exaggerated optimism that often precede market downturns. By understanding these indicators, investors can shield themselves from the pitfalls of exuberance-driven decisions and make informed choices aligned with long-term financial goals.

Historical Context: Previous Market Booms

To decipher the patterns of market exuberance, one must delve into the annals of financial history. Previous market booms serve as instructive guides, illustrating the cyclical nature of investor sentiment. The dot-com bubble of the late 1990s stands out as a stark reminder. Investors were captivated by the promise of unprecedented returns from internet-related stocks. However, the bubble burst, leading to substantial losses.

Similarly, the housing market frenzy in the mid-2000s showcased how exuberance can extend beyond the stock market. Speculative real estate investments flourished, fueled by unrealistic expectations of never-ending price escalation. When the bubble burst, triggering the global financial crisis of 2008, countless investors faced severe consequences.

By studying these historical instances, investors gain insights into the dynamics of market psychology. Recognizing the euphoria that precedes a market downturn becomes crucial for making strategic decisions. It emphasizes the importance of a balanced approach, steering clear of assets inflated by hype.

Identifying Hype in Cryptocurrencies, NFTs, and Trading Courses

In the contemporary landscape, identifying market exuberance requires a discerning eye amid the surge of cryptocurrencies, NFTs, and trading courses. Cryptocurrencies, notably Bitcoin, experienced meteoric rises, capturing the imagination of investors. The hype surrounding these digital assets often overshadows their inherent volatility and risks.

NFTs, or non-fungible tokens, entered the scene as unique digital assets, creating a fervor in the art and entertainment worlds. While some NFTs hold genuine value, the market's exuberance has led to inflated prices for digital collectibles, necessitating caution.

Trading courses, promising to unlock the secrets of financial success, have proliferated with the rise of online platforms. However, not all courses deliver on their lofty promises. Investors must distinguish between valuable educational resources and those leveraging market exuberance to sell dubious strategies.

Understanding the hype surrounding these assets and courses involves scrutinizing exaggerated claims and assessing the underlying fundamentals. Genuine opportunities withstand scrutiny, while exuberance-driven ventures often crumble under closer inspection. Chapter 1 underscores the importance of distinguishing between genuine market trends and inflated excitement, guiding investors toward prudent decision-making in a landscape rife with exuberance-driven noise.

Chapter 2: The Illusion of Quick Wealth

Chapter 2 unveils the deceptive allure of quick wealth, delving into the intricacies of get-rich-quick schemes. By dismantling the illusions surrounding rapid financial success, this chapter guides readers toward a realistic understanding of the time and effort required for sustainable prosperity.

Dissecting Get-Rich-Quick Schemes

Get-rich-quick schemes, with their seductive promises of instant affluence, often prey on the vulnerable and the hopeful. Chapter 2 dissects these schemes, exposing their fundamental flaws. Whether presented as trading systems, investment secrets, or shortcut strategies, these schemes share a common thread – a lack of substance.

One hallmark of these schemes is the emphasis on minimal effort yielding maximum gains. They market themselves as exclusive opportunities known only to a select few, creating a sense of urgency to lure individuals into hasty decisions. The truth, however, lies in the recognition that genuine wealth accumulation demands time, discipline, and a well-thought-out financial plan.

Another characteristic is the reliance on anecdotal success stories, portraying individuals who purportedly achieved immense wealth effortlessly. These narratives, while compelling, often lack verifiable evidence and serve as emotional hooks to manipulate potential investors.

Moreover, get-rich-quick schemes frequently blur the line between investing and speculation. True investing involves careful consideration of risk and a focus on long-term growth. In contrast, these schemes often encourage impulsive actions driven by the promise of immediate riches, exposing investors to unnecessary risks.

Realities of Short-Term Gains in Investing

In exploring the realities of short-term gains, Chapter 2 elucidates the distinction between investment and speculation. While certain success stories make headlines, the broader truth reveals that these instances are outliers rather than the norm. Short-term gains are elusive and unpredictable, often tied to market volatility or speculative bubbles.

Investors must recognize that attempting to time the market for quick profits is akin to gambling. The stock market's inherent unpredictability makes consistently generating short-term gains a challenging endeavor. Even professional investors with extensive experience approach short-term trading with caution due to its inherent risks.

The chapter emphasizes the importance of a realistic investment horizon. Long-term success in investing hinges on patience, diversification, and a focus on fundamental analysis. Attempting to chase short-term gains can lead to emotional decision-making and heightened vulnerability to market fluctuations.

Furthermore, the realities of short-term gains highlight the impact of transaction costs and taxes on overall returns. Frequent trading, characteristic of attempts to achieve quick wealth, can erode profits through fees and tax liabilities. Investors are urged to adopt a more strategic and measured approach that aligns with their broader financial goals.

Chapter 3: Clarifying Investment Goals

Chapter 3, "Clarifying Investment Goals," serves as a compass, guiding readers through the crucial task of defining their financial objectives. By unraveling the layers of aspirations and expectations, this chapter lays the groundwork for aligning investments with individual goals, fostering a more intentional and purpose-driven approach to wealth creation.

Defining "Rich": Long-Term Financial Independence vs. Short-Term Wealth

In the pursuit of financial prosperity, one must first unravel the subjective notion of being "rich." Chapter 3 delves into the nuanced distinction between long-term financial independence and the allure of short-term wealth.

Long-term financial independence embodies a sustainable and secure future. It signifies the ability to cover living expenses comfortably without the need for active employment income. Achieving this state requires strategic investing, prudent spending, and a commitment to long-term financial planning. It is a gradual journey, emphasizing the patient accumulation of wealth over time.

On the other hand, the allure of short-term wealth often revolves around the desire for immediate affluence and the trappings of luxury. This perspective, often fueled by societal expectations and market exuberance, tends to prioritize quick gains over the steadiness of long-term financial well-being.

Understanding this distinction is crucial for setting meaningful investment goals. It allows individuals to align their strategies with their true aspirations, avoiding the pitfalls of pursuing short-term wealth at the expense of long-term financial independence. By clarifying these goals, investors can tailor their approaches, choosing investments that resonate with their unique definitions of success.

Setting Realistic Investment Expectations

Setting realistic investment expectations is a pivotal aspect of financial success explored in Chapter 3. It involves embracing a holistic view of the investment journey, acknowledging that genuine wealth accumulation is a marathon, not a sprint.

The chapter emphasizes the importance of tempering expectations, especially in an era marked by hyperbole and exaggerated claims. While the allure of quick gains may be tempting, it's essential to ground expectations in the historical realities of investment returns. The average annual return of the S&P 500, often considered a benchmark, hovers around 10%. However, this figure must be assessed with a critical eye, considering factors like taxes and inflation that diminish the actual returns.

Realistic investment expectations encompass a recognition of the trade-offs involved. High-return opportunities often come with higher risks, and the pursuit of extraordinary gains can expose investors to volatility. By adopting a balanced perspective, investors can avoid the pitfalls of unrealistic expectations and make decisions aligned with their long-term financial goals.

Chapter 4: The Role of Saving in Wealth Building

Chapter 4 unveils the unsung hero of wealth building – saving. It's not about stashing money under the mattress but understanding how consistent, intentional saving forms the bedrock of financial success. This chapter unfolds the power of disciplined saving, laying the groundwork for a secure financial future.

Examining the Spectrum Group Survey on Net Worth

Let's peek into the Spectrum Group Survey, a treasure trove of insights into how everyday folks amass wealth. It tells us that those cruising comfortably with net worth between $100,000 and $1 million often attribute their success to a dedicated saving routine.

Imagine this: the survey asked these successful folks about the importance of a "dedicated and regular savings program." Guess what? It scored high—really high! For those climbing the ladder to a million dollars, this simple habit earned an 81.98 score in the survey. That's like getting an A+ in financial wisdom!

Now, let's dive into the millionaire zone. What did they say? Well, they cranked it up even higher! Millionaires gave it an impressive 84.14 score. And if you're talking about the ultra-rich, those with a net worth above $5 million, they were practically shouting it from the rooftops with an 85.52 score. That's like the gold medal of financial habits!

This survey is like a financial GPS, telling us that saving is a universal key to unlocking wealth. Whether you're in the hustle for your first hundred grand or eyeing the millionaire's club, a disciplined saving routine is your trusty sidekick.

Prudent Spending and Saving Habits of Successful Individuals (400 words):

Okay, let's break it down. What's the secret sauce of those successful folks who sailed smoothly into the realm of financial stability? Turns out, it's not about squeezing every dime, but about being smart with your money.

Picture this: the Spectrum Group Survey zoomed in on households with net worths between $100,000 and $1 million, asking them about the factors that fueled their success. Guess what climbed the charts? A whopping 81.98 score for the statement, "A dedicated and regular savings program is something I consider very important." Translation? These successful individuals were disciplined savers. They weren't splurging left and right; they were channeling their money into a savings routine.

Now, let's raise the stakes. What about millionaires? Well, they cranked up the financial wisdom even more. They gave the same statement an 84.14 score. And if you're talking about the ultra-rich, those with a net worth above $5 million, they practically shouted their love for saving with an 85.52 score.

It's like they were saying, "Saving money is the real MVP!"

Here's the takeaway: the successful folks weren't hoarding every penny or avoiding spending altogether. They were just smart spenders. They knew when to indulge a bit and when to tighten the purse strings. It's not about pinching pennies; it's about being mindful of where those pennies go.

So, here's the golden nugget – successful people weren't born with a silver spoon. They were born with financial smarts. They saw the value of prudent spending and embraced a dedicated savings routine. It's not rocket science; it's financial street smarts in action. And you know what? You can unleash this power too – one smart spending choice and one savings move at a time.

Chapter 5: The Power of Compound Returns

Imagine your money making little money babies, and those babies making more money babies. It's not a fairy tale; it's the real deal. This chapter peels back the curtain on how this financial superpower can turn even modest savings into a wealth-building juggernaut.

Understanding Long-Term Averages in the Stock Market

Let's dive into the stock market – not as a scary maze but as a playground for growing your money. Long-term averages, like the superhero S&P 500, show us the scorecard of how stocks perform on average over many years.

Imagine this: on this stock market playground, there's a buddy named S&P 500. Now, this buddy has a superpower – averaging around 10% return every year. That means, on average, your money can grow by 10% annually by hanging out with this superhero.

But, hold on a sec. There's a trick – taxes and inflation want a piece of the pie. So, that 10% isn't all yours. After these money-snatchers take their share, you might be left with around 5.4%. It's like sharing your ice cream, but with your money.

Realizing the Impact of Taxes and Inflation on Returns

Picture this: you've got your money in the stock market game, and it's doing its happy dance, averaging around 10% return. Sounds like a sweet deal, right? Well, here's the plot twist – taxes and inflation want a slice of your success story.

Meet the tax monster and the inflation gremlin. The tax monster chomps away a chunk of your gains. It's like paying a toll on the money highway. So, that 10% average? After taxes, it's more like 7.3%.

Now, let's talk about the inflation gremlin. It's the sneaky creature that makes your money less powerful over time. If prices go up (thanks to inflation), your money's purchasing power goes down. So, that 7.3% after taxes? After inflation, it becomes a modest 5.4%.

Why does this matter? Well, it's like trying to run a race with ankle weights. You're still moving, but not as fast. That's why understanding this tag team of taxes and inflation is crucial.

But don't let this twist get you down. It's not about avoiding the game but playing it smart. Knowing that taxes and inflation tag along, you can make strategic moves. Maybe pick investments with lower tax bites or consider investments that can outrun the inflation gremlin.

In the financial world, knowing the rules of the game can turn you from a rookie to a pro. So, when you see that 10% average return, high-five yourself for understanding the fine print. It's not just about making money; it's about keeping more of it. And that, my friend, is how you outsmart the tax monster and the inflation gremlin in this money adventure.

Chapter 6: The Myth of Overnight Success

In Chapter 6, we debunk the myth of overnight success. Forget the magic wand; building wealth is more like a steady climb than a sudden leap. This chapter unveils the truth behind those stories that make success seem like an instant potion when, in reality, it's a gradual concoction.

Analyzing Case Studies: From Zero to Hero

Ever heard those jaw-dropping tales of folks going from zero to hero overnight? Let's dissect a few. Take Bitcoin Bob, the guy who turned pocket change into millions. Sounds like a dream, right? But here's the catch – for every Bitcoin Bob, there are thousands of Bobs who didn't hit the jackpot.

Now, meet Crypto Cathy, who rode the NFT wave to fame and fortune. Impressive, no doubt. But for every Cathy, countless others got caught in the wave's undertow.

And don't forget Stock Steven, the legend who picked the perfect stocks. High-fives for Steven! Yet, for every Steven, there's an army of less fortunate stock pickers.

These tales are like shooting stars – dazzling but rare. They make headlines, but they don't tell the whole story. For every success, there are countless attempts that didn't make it to the spotlight.

Recognizing the Rare Occurrences vs. Common

Realities

Let's get real about those Cinderella stories. Sure, we've all heard about someone striking it rich overnight, whether in crypto, NFTs, or stocks. But here's the reality check – these stories are the exceptions, not the rule.

Take a stroll through the financial neighborhood, and you'll find more folks on a gradual climb than those who took an elevator straight to the top. The truth is, overnight success is as rare as finding a unicorn in your backyard.

For every crypto millionaire, there are countless others who bought in too late or got burned in the volatility. Behind every NFT sensation, there's an army of creators whose digital masterpieces are still waiting for their turn in the spotlight. And in the stock market, for every winner, there are many more who faced losses and lessons.

Why does this matter? Because believing in the overnight success myth can lead to unrealistic expectations. It's like expecting a single lottery ticket to solve all your financial puzzles. Sure, someone wins, but most walk away with just a scrap of paper.

Recognizing the rarity of these overnight tales doesn't mean shunning ambition. It means embracing a realistic perspective. Wealth-building is a journey, not a sprint. It involves learning, adapting, and, yes, facing setbacks.

Chapter 7: Balancing Saving and Investing

It's not about choosing sides but understanding how these allies can work hand in hand. This chapter guides you through the dance of dollars, where saving meets investing for a financial tango.

Debunking the Myth of Mutual Exclusivity

Let's bust a myth wide open – the idea that saving and investing are sworn enemies. It's time to clear the air and realize they're more like Batman and Robin, a dynamic duo fighting for your financial success.

Some say, "Focus only on saving, forget about investing." Others chant, "Invest all your money, who needs saving?" But here's the truth: pitting them against each other is like having a peanut butter sandwich without the jelly – it's good, but it could be so much better.

Imagine saving as the foundation – the sturdy base of your financial house. It's where you gather your financial bricks, creating a safety net for rainy days. Now, investing? Think of it as the superhero cape, swooping in to boost your wealth.

The myth of mutual exclusivity often stems from misunderstanding their roles. Saving isn't just stashing money under the mattress; it's the steady flow into your emergency fund, your safety buffer. Investing, on the other hand, is the growth engine, turning your money into a powerhouse.

Incorporating Both Elements for Financial Success

Let's play the financial harmony symphony. Saving and investing – two instruments creating a masterpiece. The key is not choosing one over the other but orchestrating a symphony where both elements harmonize for financial success.

Picture this: you're saving money, building that safety net, and then comes investing – the maestro turning your saved notes into a wealth symphony.

It's about creating a melody where your financial goals sing in unison.

But how do you strike the right chord? Start with an emergency fund – your financial anchor. Once that's set, let the investing superhero take the stage. It's not about being an investing guru but making informed decisions.

Why the combo deal? Because saving alone might feel like a cozy blanket, but without investing, your wealth might doze off. And investing without saving is like a rocket without a launchpad – it lacks stability.

Chapter 8: Evaluating Investment Opportunities

It's like putting on a detective hat to separate the gold mines from the fool's gold. This chapter equips you with tools to sift through the sea of options, making informed choices for your financial journey.

Assessing Cryptocurrencies, NFTs, and Trading Courses

Let's navigate the investment jungle and shine a light on cryptocurrencies, NFTs, and trading courses. Cryptocurrencies are like digital coins in a futuristic arcade. NFTs? Think of them as unique digital art pieces – like rare collectibles in the online world. Trading courses? They're the guidebooks promising to turn you into an investment ninja.

Now, how do you assess these opportunities without getting lost in the techno-jargon? Start with crypto – understand the technology, research the team behind it, and beware of hype-driven decisions.

NFTs? Look beyond the flashy graphics; consider the demand and authenticity.

Trading courses? Check the track record of the guru offering the secrets. Don't dive in blindfolded; ensure they've got more than just catchy slogans.

Identifying Red Flags and Exaggerated Claims

Ever seen an investment opportunity that screams "too good to be true"? Chapter 8 is your guide to spotting those red flags and deflating exaggerated claims. Whether it's a crypto promising overnight millions, an NFT that feels like a get-rich-quick scheme, or a trading course boasting guaranteed success – caution is your ally.

First, beware of promises that sound like magic spells. If it claims to turn pocket change into private jets in a blink, it's probably weaving an illusion. Second, scrutinize the storyteller – is it a seasoned expert or someone selling dreams? And third, watch out for the herd effect – just because everyone's rushing in doesn't mean it's a guaranteed gold rush.

Chapter 9: Building Sustainable Wealth

Think of it as constructing a financial fortress that weathers storms and stands tall. This chapter lays out the foundations for long-lasting financial success, emphasizing stability and resilience in your wealth journey.

Strategies for Increasing Savings

Now, let's tackle the art of boosting your savings – the cornerstone of wealth-building. Saving isn't about deprivation; it's about smart choices. Start with budgeting – a financial GPS that guides you. Track your spending, identify areas to trim, and redirect those funds into your savings account.

Next up, automate your savings. Treat it like a monthly bill – a non-negotiable commitment to your financial future. And don't forget the emergency fund; it's your financial superhero in unexpected times.

Now, let's talk about side hustles – the secret weapon to supercharge your income. Whether it's freelancing, selling handmade crafts, or driving for a rideshare service, these side gigs inject extra fuel into your savings engine.

Enhancing Investment Returns through Prudent Choices

Once your savings game is strong, it's time to amplify your investment returns through wise choices. Diving into the stock market? Think of it like a buffet – diverse options offer a balanced feast. Consider low-cost index funds, where your money mingles with a mix of stocks, spreading risks.

Explore tax-efficient strategies to keep more of your returns. Utilize retirement accounts like IRAs and 401(k)s – they're like financial fortresses shielding your gains from unnecessary tax bites.

And don't underestimate the power of patience. Let your investments marinate; it's the slow-cooking method for wealth growth. Avoid the temptation of constant tinkering; it's like opening the oven door every few minutes – the recipe won't turn out right.

Lastly, diversify like a pro. Spread your investments across various asset classes – stocks, bonds, real estate. It's like having a diverse team; when one member falters, others step up.

Chapter 10: Long-Term Financial Strategies

Chapter 10 unfolds the realm of long-term financial strategies, mapping a route beyond quick fixes. It's your GPS for sustained prosperity, emphasizing foresight, planning, and a marathon mindset. In this chapter, we'll explore strategies that extend beyond the horizon, steering your financial ship through changing tides.

The Importance of Active Income

Active income – the heartbeat of your financial health. Chapter 10 puts a spotlight on why it matters. While investments play a crucial role, active income is your reliable companion. It's the salary, the freelancing gig, the entrepreneurial venture – the income streams you actively generate.

Active income isn't just about paying bills; it's the fuel for your financial engine. It powers your savings, feeds your investments, and provides a safety net during market hiccups. Dependence solely on investments can be like sailing without a paddle – challenging.

This chapter unveils the synergy between active income and wealth-building. It's not about dismissing the allure of passive gains but recognizing the dynamic dance between what you earn actively and what your investments generate.

Diversification and Asset Allocation

Let's unravel the magic of diversification and asset allocation – not in Wall Street jargon but in plain language. Imagine your financial portfolio as a garden. Diversification is like planting various flowers – roses, tulips, and daisies. Each has its season, and together, they ensure your garden stays vibrant year-round.

Asset allocation is your gardener's wisdom, deciding how much space each flower gets. Too much of one, and your garden may tilt; too little, and some flowers may wither. Similarly, asset allocation balances your money across stocks, bonds, and other investments.

Why does this matter? Because just as flowers thrive in different conditions, assets perform differently in varying market scenarios. When stocks sway, bonds may stand firm – a natural rhythm that reduces risks.

Chapter 11: The Ethics of Financial Marketing

Chapter 11 delves into the ethical landscape of financial marketing. It's the compass navigating through the moral territories of promoting financial products. This chapter scrutinizes the principles governing how financial opportunities are presented to the public, emphasizing transparency and honesty.

Addressing Unethical Practices

Unveiling the darker corners of financial marketing, Chapter 11 addresses unethical practices that often lurk in the shadows. From exaggerated claims of overnight wealth to the manipulation of emotions, some marketing tactics resemble more of a magic show than a reliable guide to financial decisions.

Firstly, let's spotlight the "get-rich-quick" allure. Chapter 11 peels back the layers, revealing the smoke and mirrors behind promises that seem too good to be true. Whether it's cryptocurrencies, NFTs, or trading courses, caution is the watchword. By dissecting these promises, readers gain a clearer view of the risks and realities.

Emotional manipulation, a covert player in financial marketing, also takes center stage. Techniques designed to trigger fear, greed, or urgency can lead individuals into hasty decisions. Chapter 11 dismantles these manipulative strategies, empowering readers to make decisions based on rational analysis rather than emotional impulses.

The Need for Improved Regulations

As the curtain lifts on unethical practices, Chapter 11 advocates for the need for improved regulations in the financial marketing arena. While some boundaries exist, they often resemble more of a picket fence than a fortress. Strengthening these barriers becomes crucial in safeguarding consumers from misleading campaigns.

Consider the comparison between traditional financial advisors and the influencers promoting speculative assets. Financial advisors undergo rigorous regulations, ensuring they provide accurate information and act in the client's best interest. However, the digital realm lacks such stringent oversight, allowing for a wild west of unchecked claims.

Chapter 11 navigates through the gaps in existing regulations, emphasizing the urgency to adapt to the evolving landscape. It argues for a balance where innovation thrives but not at the cost of consumer vulnerability. Stricter scrutiny on how financial products are marketed, especially those with high-risk propositions, becomes imperative.

The role of influencers in financial marketing receives a spotlight, questioning the ethical responsibility they carry. Influencers, often with vast followings, possess the power to sway financial decisions. Chapter 11 advocates for transparency, urging influencers to disclose conflicts of interest and avoid promoting products solely for personal gains.

In conclusion, Chapter 11 serves as a call to action – a plea for a more ethical and regulated financial marketing sphere. It envisions a landscape where individuals can navigate financial opportunities with confidence, knowing that the information presented aligns with reality. Through a combination of awareness, consumer education, and regulatory enhancements, this chapter aims to foster an environment where financial marketing serves as a trustworthy guide rather than a treacherous labyrinth.

CONCLUSION

In this comprehensive book, the author embarks on a journey to demystify the allure of quick wealth through various investment opportunities, including cryptocurrencies, NFTs, and trading courses. The narrative begins by revisiting the rampant market exuberance, emphasizing the risks associated with get-rich-quick schemes prevalent in the financial space. Drawing on historical context, the author explores previous market booms, highlighting the transient nature of extraordinary returns.

The book serves as a critical guide to navigating the current landscape of hype-driven investments. It meticulously dissects the illusion of quick wealth, addressing the deceptive tactics employed by influencers and promoters. It underscores the importance of recognizing the limitations of investing, debunking the notion that it can swiftly transform one's financial situation.

Chapters unfold to clarify investment goals, distinguish between long-term financial independence and short-term wealth, and set realistic expectations for returns. The author emphasizes the pivotal role of savings in wealth-building, drawing insights from a Spectrum Group Survey on net worth. The narrative is anchored in the power of compound returns, unraveling the impact of taxes and inflation on investment outcomes.

As the book progresses, it advocates for sustainable wealth-building strategies, including increasing savings through prudent choices and enhancing investment returns. It underscores the significance of active income alongside investments and elucidates the concepts of diversification and asset allocation in accessible language.

In the final chapters, the book delves into the ethics of financial marketing, addressing unethical practices and advocating for improved regulations. It critically evaluates the promises made by influencers and the need for transparency in financial promotions.

In conclusion, the book provides a holistic guide to financial decision-making, debunking myths, clarifying realities, and instilling a sense of financial responsibility. It empowers readers to approach investments with a discerning eye, urging them to prioritize sustainable strategies over the allure of overnight success. Through a blend of historical insights, practical advice, and ethical considerations, the book equips individuals with the tools to navigate the complex landscape of personal finance.